for walkers

South West Coast Path
North Devon & Somerset

T0337709

▨ This publication covers the North Devon & Somerset section of the South West Coast Path, a National Trail extending 630 miles from Minehead in Somerset to Poole Harbour in Dorset and including a great variety of landscape, wildlife and geology.

▨ Containing Ordnance Survey maps in a convenient book format with an index to the main features, each of the five books show all footpaths, rights of way and public access land, and are the essential companion whether tackling the entire route or enjoying a relaxing afternoon walk in North Devon or Somerset.

CONTENTS

Reference / Legend.................2-3
Key to Map Pages...................4-7
Map Pages...........................8-43
Index...................................44-47
Route Planner...........................48

Ferries.......................................49
Tourist Information....................49
Safety & Security......................51
QR codes............................52-53

A-Z AtoZ

registered trade marks of
Geographers' A-Z Map Company Ltd

www./az.co.uk

EDITION 3 2019
Copyright © Geographers' A-Z Map Company Ltd.

© Crown copyright and database rights 2019. Ordnance Survey 100017302.

1:25 000 maps are sourced from Ordnance Survey.
Public rights of way shown on these maps have been taken from local authority definitive maps and later amendments.
The representation on the maps of any other road, track or footpath is no evidence of the existence of a right of way.

© National Trail logos and material are reproduced with the permission of Walk Unlimited Ltd.

Communications and Access

ROADS AND PATHS
Not necessarily rights of way

Service areas	**7** Junction number	**T1** Toll road junction

M 1 or A 6(M)	Motorway
A35	Dual carriageway
A30	Main road
B3074	Secondary road
	Narrow road with passing places
	Road under construction
	Road generally more than 4m wide
	Road generally less than 4m wide
	Other road, drive or track, fenced and unfenced
	Gradient: steeper than 20% (1 in 5); 14% (1 in 7) to 20% (1 in 5)
Ferry	Ferry; Ferry P (passenger only)
	⊕ London River Services
	Path

RAILWAYS

Single track   Station, open to passengers   Siding

Standard gauge

Multiple track   ⊖ London Underground

| Road over | Road under | Level crossing | Cutting | Embankment |

Tunnel

Station

Narrow gauge, tramway or light rail system

PUBLIC RIGHTS OF WAY
Rights of way are not shown on maps of Scotland

- - - - - - - - - Footpath   — — — — — Bridleway

+-+-+-+-+- Byway open to all traffic

-+--+--+--+- Restricted byway (not for use by mechanically propelled vehicles)

Public rights of way shown on OS maps have been taken from local authority definitive maps and later amendments. Rights of way are liable to change and may not be clearly defined on the ground. Please check with the relevant local authority for the latest information.
The representation on this map of any other road, track or path is no evidence of the existence of a right of way

PUBLIC ACCESS (Scotland)

In Scotland, everyone has access rights in law (Land Reform Scotland Act 2003) over most land and inland water, provided access is exercised responsibly. This includes walking, cycling, horse-riding and water access, for recreational and educational purposes, and for crossing land or water.
Access rights do not cover to motorised activities, hunting, shooting or fishing, nor if your dog is not under proper control.
The Scottish Outdoor Access Code is the reference point for responsible behaviour, and can be obtained at www.outdooraccess-scotland.com or by phoning your local Scottish Natural Heritage office.

National Trust for Scotland

 always open

limited access, observe local signs

Forestry Commission Land, normally open, observe local signs

Woodland Trust Land

OTHER PUBLIC ACCESS

• • • •   Other routes with public access (not normally shown in urban areas)

The exact nature of the rights on these routes and the existence of any restrictions may be checked with the local highway authority. Alignments are based on the best information available.

◆ ◆   Recreational route (◇ alternative route)
○ One mile distance marker

◆——◆   South West Coast Path

National Trail   Scotland's Great Trails

- - - - - - Permissive footpath   — — — Permissive bridleway

Footpaths and bridleways along which landowners have permitted public use but which are not rights of way. The agreement may be withdrawn.

• • • •   Traffic-free cycle route

1 **1**   National cycle network route number - traffic free; on road

Firing and test ranges in the area. Danger! Observe warning notices

Access permitted within managed controls, for example, local byelaws

For more information:
www.gov.uk/guidance/public-access-to-military-areas

Ministry of Defence (MOD) Area - Purbeck & South Dorset

— — —   Range walks

— • — •   Roads open when range walks open

Range walk starting point

ACCESS LAND (England and Wales)

Access land portrayed on this map is intended as a guide to land normally available for access on foot, for example access land created under the Countryside and Rights of Way Act 2000, and land managed by National Trust, Forestry Commission, Woodland Trust and Natural Resources Wales. Some restrictions will apply; some land shown as access land may not have open access rights; always refer to local signage.

Eastbourne & Beachy Head

i Access info. point

Point of access to the foreshore

Access land

within woodland area

within sand

The depiction of rights of access does not imply or express any warranty as to its accuracy or completeness. Observe local signs and follow the Countryside Code.

Visit gov.uk/government/publications/the-countryside-code

Coastal margin

All land within the 'coastal margin' (where it already exists) is associated with the England Coast Path (nationaltrail.co.uk/england-coast-path) and is by default access land,but in some areas it contains land not subject to access rights - for example cropped land, buildings and their curtilage, gardens and land subject to local restriction including many areas of saltmarsh and flat that are not suitable for public access. The coastal margin is often steep, unstable and not readily accessible. Please take careful note of conditions and local signage on the ground

Scale 1:25 000

1 Kilometre = 0.6214 mile
1 metre = 3.2808 feet

1 mile = 1.6093 kilometres
100 feet = 30.48 metres

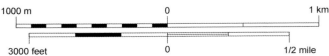

1000 m   0   1 km

3000 feet   0   1/2 mile

3

General Information

BOUNDARIES

— + — + — National — · — · — County; England

— — — Unitary Authority (UA), London Borough (LB), Metropolitan District (Met Dist) or District

(Scotland & Wales are solely Unitary Authorities)

· · · · · · · · · · · · Civil Parish (CP); England or Community (C); Wales

▬▬▬ National Park boundary

VEGETATION

Limits of vegetation are defined by positioning of symbols

Coniferous trees   Non-coniferous trees   Coppice

Bracken, heath or rough grassland   Orchard

Marsh, reeds or saltings   Scrub

GENERAL FEATURES

Gravel pit   Sand pit

Other pit or quarry   Landfill site or slag/spoil heap

pylon pole   Electricity transmission line

Solar farm

Slopes

+ Place of worship

Current or former place of worship

with tower

with spire, minaret or dome

△ Triangulation pillar

Ⱦ Mast

✗ Windmill, with or without sails

Ⴗ Wind pump

Wind turbine

▭ ▭ Building; important building

⊠ Glasshouse

▲ Youth hostel

▬ Bunkhouse, camping barn or other hostel

Bus or coach station

Lighthouse; disused lighthouse; beacon

ABBREVIATIONS

BP/BS	Boundary post/stone
CG	Cattle grid
CH	Clubhouse
F Sta	Fire station
FB	Footbridge
Ind Est	Industrial estate
Liby;Mkt	Library; Market
Meml	Memorial
MP;MS	Milepost; Milestone
Mon	Monument
PO	Post office
Pol Sta	Police station
Resr	Reservoir
Sch;TH	School; Town hall
NTL	Normal tidal limit
Wks	Works
W; Spr	Well; Spring

ARCHAEOLOGICAL AND HISTORICAL INFORMATION

⚜ Site of antiquity

⚔ 1066 Site of battle (with date)

☆ Visible earthwork

VILLA Roman

Castle Non-Roman

Information sourced from Historic England, Historic Environment Scotland and the Royal Commission on the Ancient and Historical Monuments of Wales.

HEIGHTS AND NATURAL FEATURES

Water

Mud

Sand

Shingle

Survey height;
52 · Ground
284 · Air

The Contour interval on 1:25 000 maps are shown at 5m and/or 10m vertical interval, to provide the most detailed heighting available.

Contours   Vertical face/cliff   Outcrop

5m   10m   Scree   Loose rock   Boulders

Surface heights are to the nearest metre above mean sea level. Where two heights are shown, the first is the height of the natural ground in the location of the triangulation pillar, and the second (in brackets) to a seperate point which is the highest natural summit.

Tourist & Leisure Information

Art gallery (notable / important)	Electric boat charging point	National Trust	Recreation, leisure or sports centre
Boat hire	English Heritage	Nature reserve	Slipway
Boat trips	Fishing	Other tourist feature	Theme or pleasure park
Building of historic interest	Forestry Commission visitor centre	Parking	Viewpoint
Cadw (Welsh Heritage)	Garden or arboretum	Park & ride, all year	Visitor centre
Camp site	Golf course or links	Park & ride, seasonal	Walks or trails
Camping and caravan site	Heritage centre	Roman site	Water activities
Caravan site	Historic Scotland	Telephone, public	Water activities (board)
Castle or fort	Horse riding	roadside assistance	Water activities (paddle)
Cathedral or abbey	Information centre	emergency	Water activities (powered)
Country park	Information centre, seasonal	Picnic site	Water activities (sailing)
Craft centre	Moorings (free)	Preserved railway	Watersports centre (multi-activity)
Cycle hire	Mountain bike trail	Public house(s)	Windmill open to public
Cycle trail	Museum	PC Public toilets	World Heritage site / area

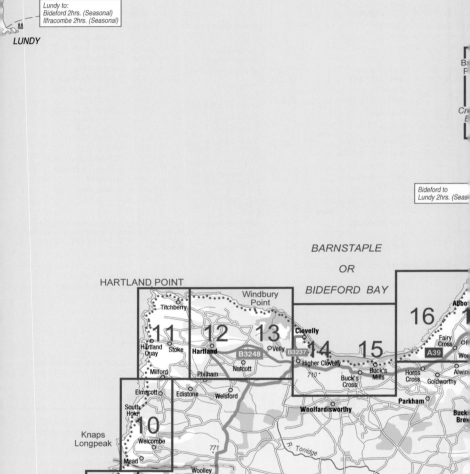

LUNDY

Lundy to:
Bideford 2hrs. (Seasonal)
Ilfracombe 2hrs. (Seasonal)

Bideford to
Lundy 2hrs. (Seas

BARNSTAPLE

OR

BIDEFORD BAY

HARTLAND POINT

Windbury
Point

Titchberry

11

Hartland
Quay   Stoke

12

Hartland

13

Clovelly

Velly

14   **15**

Abbo

16

Fairy
Cross

A39

Wo

Milford

B3248   B3237

Philham   Nattcott

Higher Clovelly

710 *

Buck's
Mills

Horns
Cross   Goldworthy

Alwin

Elmscott

Edistone   Welsford

Buck's
Cross

Parkham

Buck
Brew

South
Hole

10

Woolfardisworthy

Knaps
Longpeak

Welcombe

771

R. Torridge

Mead

Woolley

Gooseham

Morwenstow

Eastcott

Higher Sharpnose
Point

9

Shop

Woodford

A39

Upper
Tamar Lake

Bradworthy

Bulkworthy

Lower Sharpnose
Point

CORNWALL   DEVON

R   Sutcombe

Coombe

Kilkhampton

Lower
Tamar Lake

Waldon

Milton
Damerel

Stibb

B3254

A388

8

Poughill

Flexbury

Bude

Stratton

Cookbury

*Bude
Bay*

Lynstone

A3072

Holsworthy

Upton

Marhamchurch   Bridgerule   Pyworthy

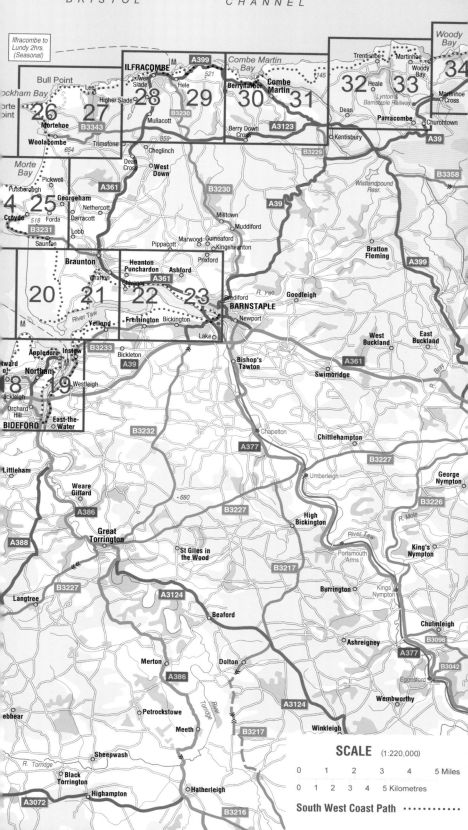

5

BRISTOL   CHANNEL

Ilfracombe to Lundy 2hrs. (Seasonal)

26 Bull Point
27
28 ILFRACOMBE
29
A399
521
Combe Martin Bay
145
30 Berrynarbor
Combe Martin
31
32 Trentishoe
Heale
Dean
33 Martinhoe
Woody Bay
Martinhoe Cross
34 Woody Bay
Churchtown
Parracombe
Lynton & Barnstaple Railway
Kentisbury

Lee
Lower Slade
Hele
Higher Slade
Mullacott
B3230
859
Berry Down Cross
A3123
A39
B3229
A39
B3358
A399
A39

Bull Point
Mortehoe
Woolacombe
Trimstone
Dean Cross
West Down
Cheglinch
Wistlandpound Resr.
Bratton Fleming

B3343
654

Morte Bay
Putsborough
Pickwell
Georgeham
Nethercott
Darracott
Lobb
Saunton
A361
Marwood
Guineaford
Kingsheanton
Prixford
Pippacott
Milltown
Muddiford
B3230

4 Croyde
25 518 Forda
B3231

20
21 Wrafton
Velland
22 Heanton Punchardon
Chivenor
Fremington
23 Bradiford
Bickington
Lake
A361
R. Yeo
Goodleigh
BARNSTAPLE
Newport

8 Appledore
Instow
Northam
19 Westleigh
BIDEFORD
Orchard Hill
East-the-Water
B3233
Bickleton
A39
Bishop's Tawton
A361
Swimbridge
West Buckland
East Buckland
R. Bray

Littleham
Weare Giffard
A386
Great Torrington
St Giles in the Wood
B3232
Chapelton
A377
Chittlehampton
Umberleigh
B3227
George Nympton
B3226
R. Mole

A388
A386
680
B3227
High Bickington
River Taw
King's Nympton
Portsmouth Arms
Kings Nympton
A377
Chulmleigh
B3096

Langtree
B3227
A3124
Beaford
B3217
Burrington
Ashreigney

Merton
Dolton
A386
A3124
Wembworthy
B3042
Eggesford

Petrockstowe
Meeth
River Torridge
B3217
Winkleigh

ebbear
Sheepwash
R. Torridge
Black Torrington
Highampton
Hatherleigh
A3072
B3216

SCALE (1:220,000)

0   1   2   3   4   5 Miles

0 1 2 3 4 5 Kilometres

South West Coast Path ●●●●●●●●●●●

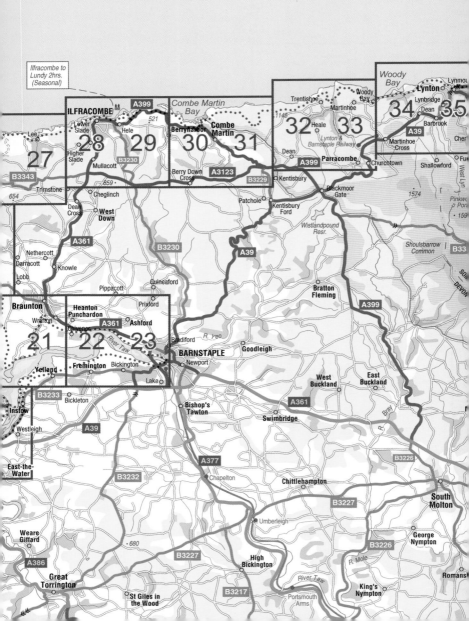

B R I S T O L

Ilfracombe to
Lundy 2hrs.
(Seasonal)

Woody
Bay

LYNTON Lynmou

34 Lynbridge
Dean
Barbrook

35

A39

Martinhoe
Cross

Cher

Shallowford

Fu

Trentishoe

Woody
Bay

Martinhoe

32 Heale

Lynton &
Barnstaple Railway

33

West Lyn

Pinkwo
o Pool

·159

Dean

A399 **Parracombe**

Churchtown

1145

1574

ILFRACOMBE A399

Lower
Slade
Hele

521

Combe Martin
Bay

Berrynarbor **Combe
Martin**

28 **29** **30** **31**

Higher
Slade

B3230

Mullacott

Dean

Kentisbury

Blackmoor
Gate

B33

Shoulsbarrow
Common

SO
DEVON

27

B3343

654

Trimstone

859

Cheglinch

**West
Down**

Dean
Cross

Berry Down
Cross

A3123

B3229

Patchole

Kentisbury
Ford

Wistlandpound
Resr.

A361

Nethercott

Darracott

Knowle

Lobb

Pippacott

Guineaford

Prixford

B3230

A39

Bratton
Fleming

A399

Braunton

Wrafton

21

Yelland

Heanton
Punchardon

Chivenor

22 **23**

A361

Ashford

Fremington

Bickington

Lake

Bradiford

R. Yeo

BARNSTAPLE

Newport

Goodleigh

West
Buckland

East
Buckland

R. Bray

B3233

Bickleton

A39

Instow

Westleigh

East-the-
Water

B3232

**Bishop's
Tawton**

Swimbridge

A361

A377

Chapelton

B3226

Chittlehampton

B3227

**South
Molton**

Weare
Giffard

·680

B3227

A386

**Great
Torrington**

St Giles in
the Wood

B3217

High
Bickington

River Taw

Portsmouth
Arms

R. Mole

B3226

George
Nympton

**King's
Nympton**

Romans

Umberleigh

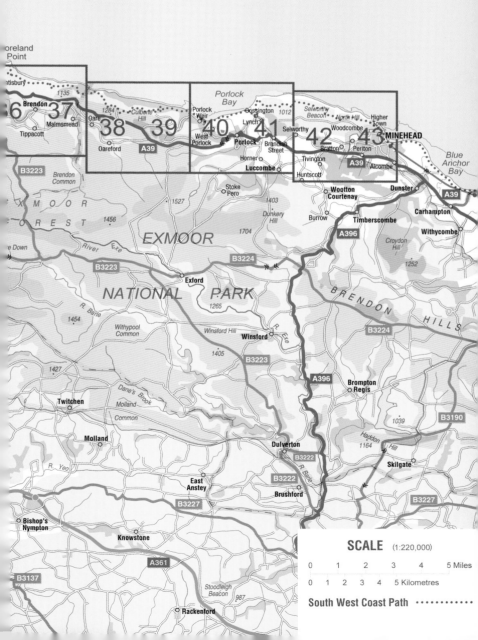

7

St Donat's Llantwit Major Llantwit Major St Athan

Nash Point

Breaksea Point

B4265

C H A N N E L

oreland Point

atisbury

Brendon 1135

Malmsmead

Tippacott

B3223

Brendon Common

36 37

1284 Culbone Hill

Oare

Oareford A39

38 39

Porlock Weir Dosgington 1012

Porlock Bay

Lynch

West Porlock

Porlock

Brandish Street

Horner

Luccombe

Selworthy Beacon North Hill

Selworthy Woodcombe Higher Town

40 41 42 43 MINEHEAD

Tivington

Huntscott

Bratton Periton

A39 Alcombe

Blue Anchor Bay

Stoke Pero

1527 1403

Dunkery Hill

Wootton Courtenay

Dunster

A39

1704

Burrow

Timberscombe

Carhampton

Withycombe

X M O O R

F O R E S T

1456

River Exe

Croydon Hill 1252

E X M O O R

B3223

A396

N A T I O N A L P A R K

B3224

B R E N D O N

H I L L S

Exford

1265

R. Barle

1454

Withypool Common

Winsford Hill

Winsford

1405

B3223

R. Exe

B3224

e Down

A396

1039

B3190

1427

Dane's Brook

Molland Common

Twitchen

Brompton Regis

Haddon Hill 1164

Molland

R. Yeo

Dulverton

B3222 R. Barle

Skilgate

B3222

East Anstey

B3227

Brushford

B3227

Bishop's Nympton

Knowstone

A361

B3137

Stoodleigh Beacon 987

Rackenford

SCALE (1:220,000)

0 1 2 3 4 5 Miles

0 1 2 3 4 5 Kilometres

South West Coast Path ··········

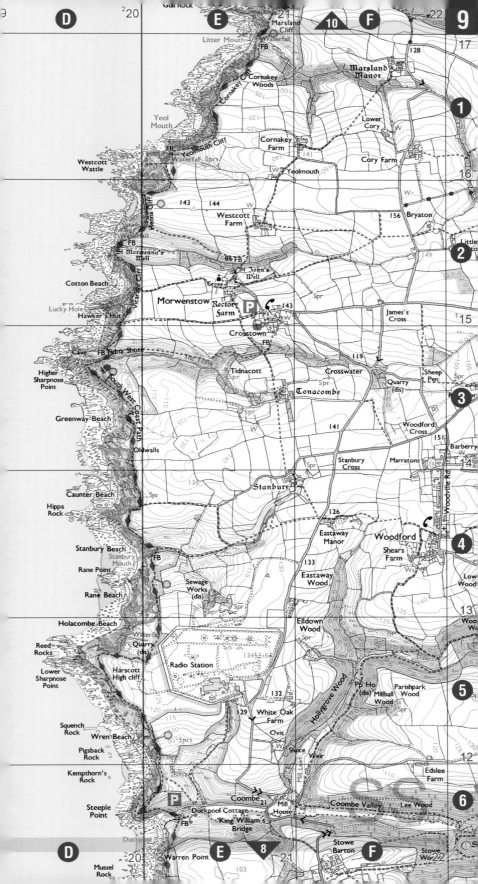

Barnstaple   or   Bideford Bay

The Gore   Gauter Point

uck's Down   24

Worthygate Wood   Slo

ord

Keivill's Wood

Sewage
Works   Gauter
                                         Pool   171   4

Bideford Bay   Higher
Holiday Park   Buck's   Worthygate
                            Wood
Buck's   175
Barton   ¡77   Buck's Mills

                                                Lower   23
                                                Worthygate   151

A 39   PO   W

Buck's   Lower
Cross   Waytown

              Cerny   Higher
North   W   Waytown
Bitworthy   Walland   Acad
                    Farm   203   5
       208   Swanton   200
                                 Farm   190
itworthy Farm   Garden   ¡91   Spr   196 W   180 Limebury
                    Centre   165
                                                             22
              Galloping Lane   W
                                                         River
Cranford   6

nford   edborough
ater   Satchfield   ²35   201   36   ¡87   F   37

16

37 Ⓐ 38 Ⓑ 39 Ⓒ

29

Ⓘ

28

Barnstaple or
Bideford Bay

Ⓘ

27

Ⓘ

26

Babbacombe Mouth

Wescott Cliff
Ford

Ⓘ Babbacombe Cliff

Ⓘ 15 Rowden Gut

25 Higher Rowden ALWINGTON CP

The Rowden Kennel Copse

Portledge

Ⓘ South West Coast Path

Chiddleco

Peppercombe Castle Ford

24 Sloo Wood Peppercombe Gilscott Spr

Ⓘ Peppercombe Cottage Northway A 39

Higher Worthyg Sloo 180 169 Spanny Hone

Ⓐ 38 Ⓑ 151 39 Sewage Works Ⓒ

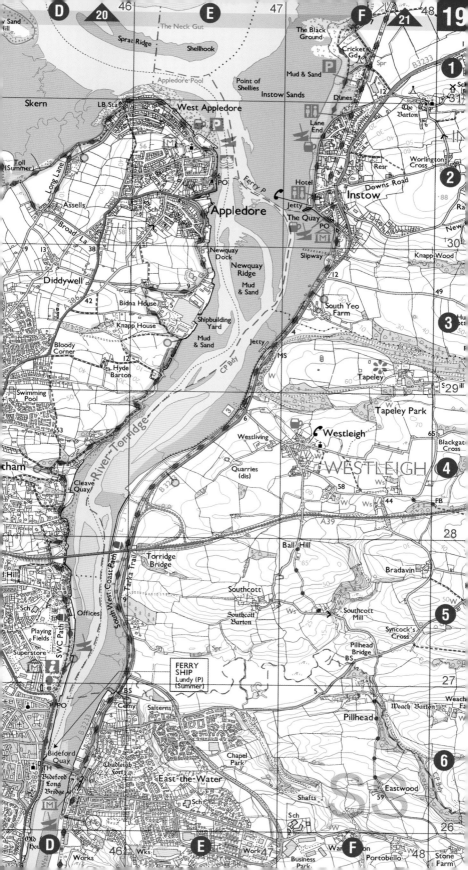

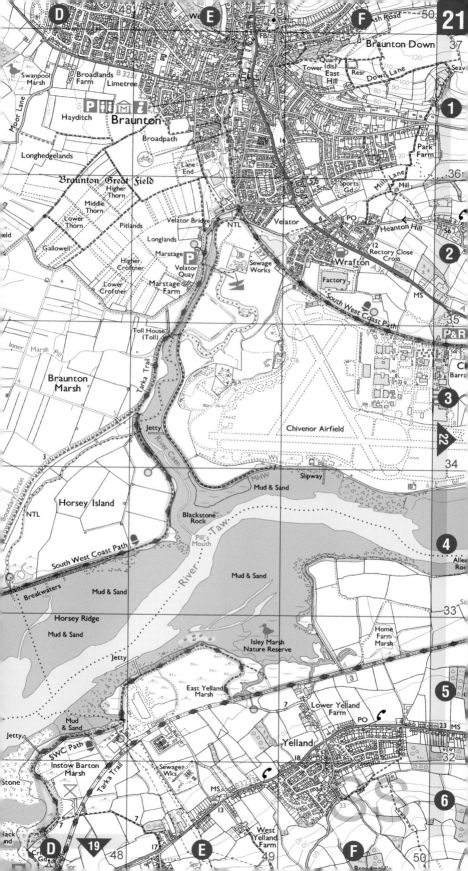

Braunton Down

Braunton

Swanpool Marsh

Broadlands Farm

Limetree

Haydiltch

Moor Lane

Longhedgelands

Broadpath

Lane End

Braunton Great Field

Higher Thorn

Middle Thorn

Lower Thorn

Pitlands

Gallowell

Velator Bridge

Longlands

Marstage

Higher Croftner

Lower Croftner

Velator Quay

Marstage Farm

Toll House (Toll)

Inner Marsh Pill

Tarka Trail

Braunton Marsh

Jetty

River Caen

Horsey Island

NTL

South West Coast Path

Breakwaters

Horsey Ridge

Mud & Sand

Mud & Sand

Jetty

Boundary Drain

Quarry (dis)

Tower

East Hill

Down Lane

Resr

Park Farm

Mill Lane

Mill

Velator

Heanton Hill

PO

Wrafton

Rectory Close Cross

Factory

MS

South West Coast Path

P&R

Chivenor Airfield

Barra

22

Slipway

Mud & Sand

MHW

Blackstone Rock

Pill's Mouth

River Taw

Mud & Sand

Mud & Sand

Isley Marsh Nature Reserve

Home Farm Marsh

Allen Roc

East Yelland Marsh

Lower Yelland Farm

PO

Yelland

Jetty

SWC Path

Instow Barton Marsh

Tarka Trail

Sewage Wks

MS

West Yelland Farm

Broadsmit

19

NTL

Sewage Works

Sch

Cei

Sch

Sports Gd

FB

B 3231

1

2

3

4

5

6

D

E

F

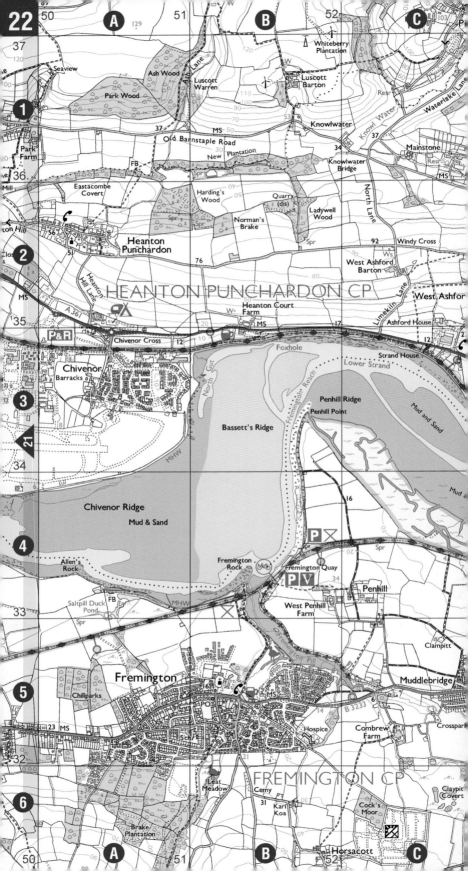

24

41 **A** 42 **B** 43 **C**

1
42

Morte Bay

2

Wheeler's Stone

Whiting
Hole
41
Long Rock
94
South West Coast Path
Cave
Tarka Trail
Baggy Point
95
90
78
100
3
98
06
80
70
Croydehoe
Farm
Pencil
Rock
60
Spr
50
40
09
Spr
78
Middleborough
Hill
P **Croyde
Bay**
4
P
Tarka Trail
Dunes
MLW
MHW
Croyde Bay
Croyde
Sand
Croyde
Burrows
Dunes
39
Down End
Croyde Road
P
5
Downend
House
Sprs
Spr
113
Chesil Cliff
House
South West Coast Path
Sa
38
B 3231

6

37
41 **A** 42 **B** 43 **C**

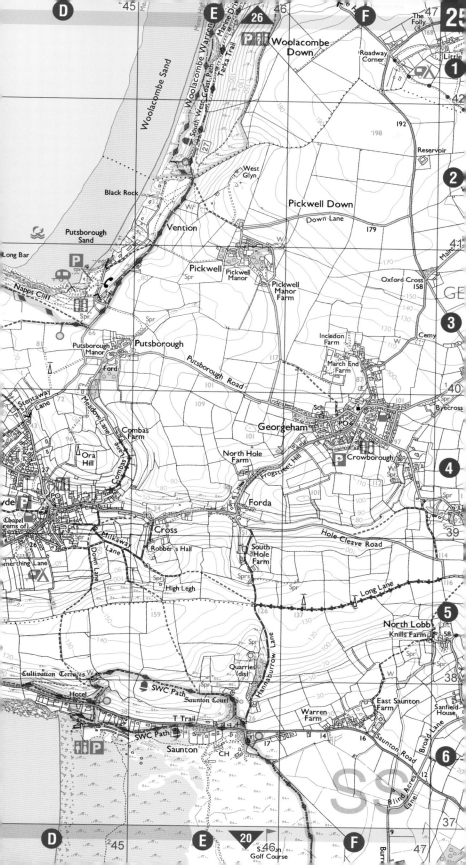

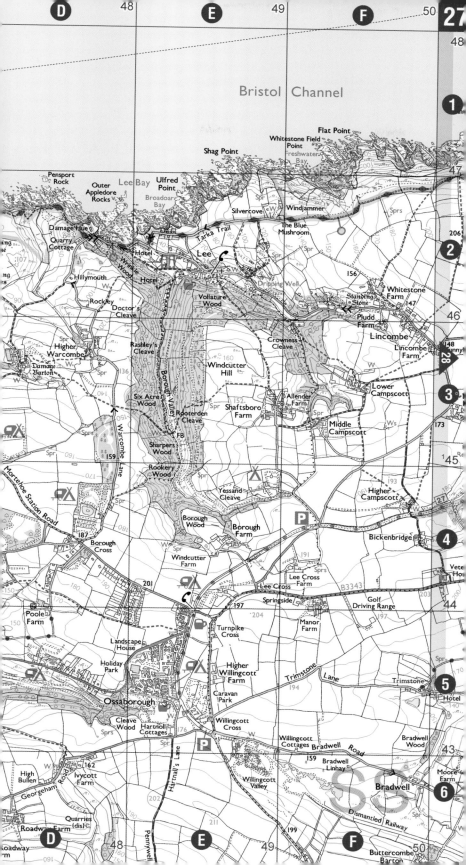

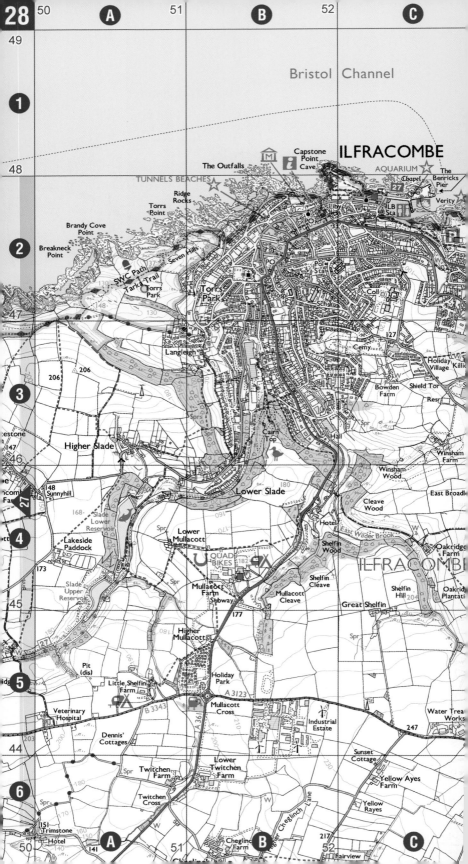

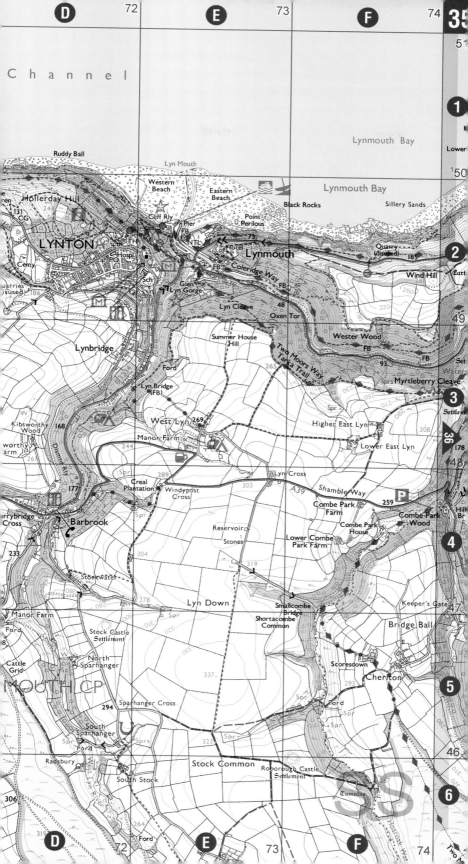

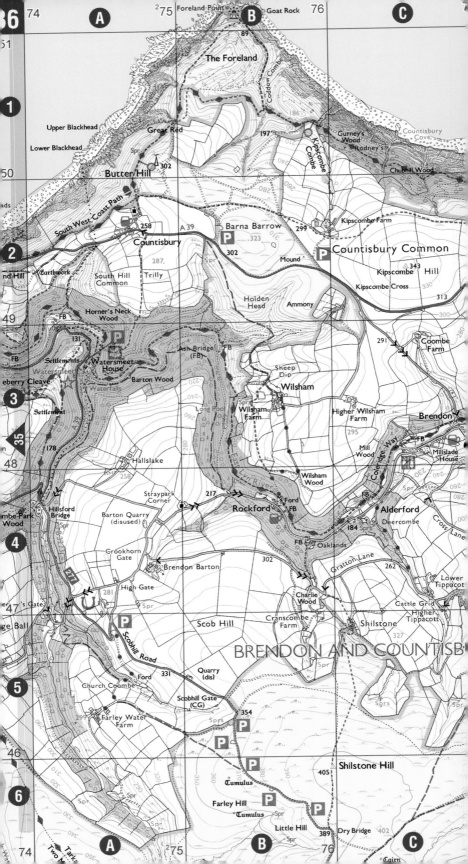

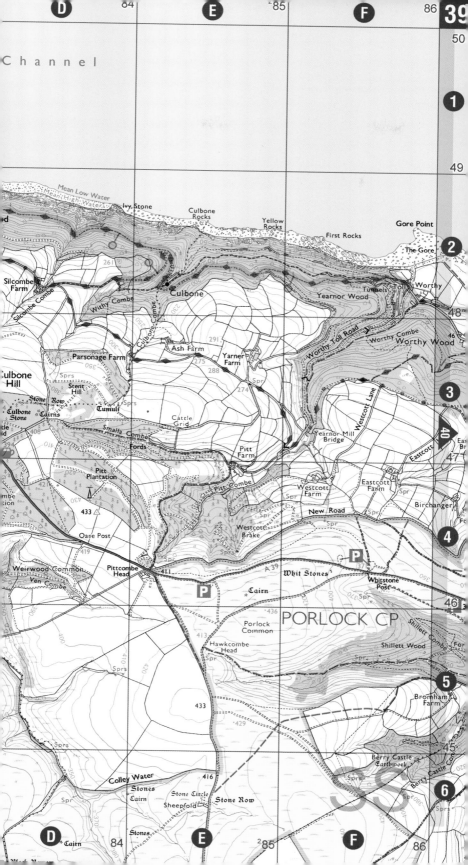

1. The map reference given refers to the actual square in which the feature is located and not the name.

2. A strict alphabetical order is used e.g. Eastcott Bridge follows East Cleave but precedes East Down Cross

3. Names prefixed with 'The' are indexed under the main name, for example 'The Beacon' appears in the B section.

THE NATIONAL GRID REFERENCING SYSTEM

The grid lines form part of the National Grid and are at 1 km intervals.

To give a unique reference position of a point to within 100 metres proceed as follows:

Sample point: **Abbotsham**

1. Read letters identifying 100,000 metre square in which the point lies (**SS**)

2. FIRST QUOTE EASTINGS - locate the first VERTICAL grid line to LEFT of the point and read the BLUE figures labelling the line in the top or bottom margin of the page (**42**). Estimate tenths from the grid line to the point (**4**). This gives a figure of **424**

3. THEN QUOTE NORTHINGS - locate the first HORIZONTAL grid line BELOW the point and read the BLUE figures labelling the line in the left or right margin of the page (**26**). Estimate tenths from the grid line to the point (**4**). This gives a figure of **264**

Sample Reference: **Abbotsham SS 424 264**

Abbotsham . . . . .6A 18 SS 424 264
Abbotsham Cliff . . . . .2D 17 SS 408 274
Abbotsham Cross . . . . .4F 17 SS 421 255
Abington Cross . . . . .3D 41 SS 895 475
Airy Point . . . . .4A 20 SS 449 330
Alcombe . . . . .5F 43 SS 973 453
Allerford . . . . .4E 41 SS 904 469
Allerford Car Park . . . . . . .4E 41 SS 904 469
Allerford Museum . . . . . . .4E 41 SS 904 469
Appledore . . . . .2E 19 SS 464 305
Appledore Bridge . . . . . . .2D 19 SS 451 304
Appledore, Churchfields Car Park
. . . . .2E 19 SS 464 307
Appledore Instow Ferry . . .2E 19 SS 468 302
Appledore Lifeboat Station
. . . . .2D 19 SS 459 309
Ash Bridge . . . . .3B 36 SS 752 487
Ashford . . . . .2D 23 SS 533 353

Babbacombe Cliff . . . . . . .4C 16 SS 393 254
Babbacombe Mouth . . . . . .4C 16 SS 392 256
Baggy Point . . . . .3A 24 SS 418 406
Baggy Point Car Park . . . . .4C 24 SS 432 397
Barbrook . . . . .4D 35 SS 715 476
Barham Hill . . . . .6C 34 SS 705 458
Barley Bay . . . . .1E 11 SS 233 277
Barna Barrow . . . . .2B 36 SS 754 495
Barna Barrow Car Park . . .2B 36 SS 752 496
Barnstaple . . . . .4F 23 SS 559 333
Barnstaple Bay . . . . .1E 15 SS 353 268
Barnstaple Station . . . . . . .5F 23 SS 555 325
Barnstaple Tourist Information Centre
. . . . .5F 23 SS 558 329
Barricane Beach . . . . .4B 26 SS 452 443
Baxworthy Cross . . . . .6D 13 SS 283 223
Beacon Point . . . . .1D 29 SS 532 482
The Beacon (Roman Fortlet)
. . . . .1E 33 SS 663 493
Beckland Bay . . . . .2D 13 SS 282 269
Beckland Cliff . . . . .2D 13 SS 283 265
Beckland Cross . . . . .3C 12 SS 277 256
Berry Down . . . . .6A 30 SS 567 436
Berrydown Cross . . . . .5B 30 SS 573 441
Berry Down Cross . . . . . . .6B 30 SS 571 437
Berrynarbor . . . . .3A 30 SS 560 466
Berrynarbor, Castle Hill Car Park
. . . . .3A 30 SS 561 466
Bickington . . . . .5D 23 SS 533 324
Bideford . . . . .6C 18 SS 445 265
Bideford Bay . . . . .1E 15 SS 356 268
Bideford Long Bridge . . . .6D 19 SS 455 264
Bideford Quay . . . . .6D 19 SS 454 265
Bideford Railway Heritage Centre
. . . . .6D 19 SS 456 263
Bideford Tourist Information Centre
. . . . .6D 19 SS 454 269
Bight a Doubleyou . . . . . . .3B 14 SS 324 244
Big Sheep . . . . .6A 18 SS 426 264
Birchanger Bridge . . . . . . .4A 40 SS 863 467
Blackchurch Rock . . . . . . .2E 13 SS 298 266
Black Gate Car Park . . . . . .3E 37 SS 788 489
Blackgate Cross . . . . .4F 19 SS 480 287
The Black Ground . . . . . . .1F 19 SS 471 314
Black Hill . . . . .6B 38 SS 816 449
Blackstone Beach . . . . . . .1D 31 SS 597 483
Blackstone Point . . . . .1E 31 SS 602 485
Blagdon Cliff . . . . .1D 11 SS 229 272
Blegberry Beach . . . . .2D 11 SS 224 260
Blegberry Cliff . . . . .2D 11 SS 225 262
Bodley . . . . .5E 33 SS 666 451
Bonhill Bridge . . . . .3A 34 SS 685 482
Bonhill Top . . . . .3A 34 SS 688 487
Borough Cross . . . . .4D 27 SS 476 444
Borough Valley . . . . .3E 27 SS 481 456

Borough Valley (Lee Bridge) Car Park
. . . . .4F 27 SS 491 445
Bossington . . . . .3D 41 SS 898 479
Bossington Beach . . . . . . .2C 40 SS 886 482
Bossington Car Park . . . . .2D 41 SS 897 480
Bossington Hill . . . . .2E 41 SS 903 484
Bossington Hill Car Park
. . . . .3F 41 SS 910 476
Bradiford . . . . .3F 23 SS 550 342
Bradwell . . . . .6F 27 SS 498 428
Brandish Street . . . . .4E 41 SS 907 466
Brandy Cove Point . . . . . . .2A 28 SS 504 475
Bratton . . . . .4C 42 SS 946 461
Bratton Ball . . . . .3C 42 SS 944 473
Braunton . . . . .1E 21 SS 487 366
Braunton & District Museum
. . . . .1E 21 SS 486 365
Braunton, Broad Sands (Crow Point) Car Park
. . . . .5C 20 SS 467 327
Braunton Burrows . . . . . . .2A 20 SS 448 350
Braunton Burrows (Sandy Lane) Car Park
. . . . .3C 20 SS 463 349
Braunton, Caen Street Car Park
. . . . .1E 21 SS 486 365
Braunton Down . . . . .1F 21 SS 496 368
Braunton Great Field . . . . .2D 21 SS 477 359
Braunton Marsh . . . . .3D 21 SS 475 345
Braunton Marsh (Velator Quay) Car Park
. . . . .2E 21 SS 484 354
Braunton Tourist Information Centre
. . . . .1E 21 SS 487 365
Breakneck Point . . . . .2A 28 SS 502 474
Brendon . . . . .3C 36 SS 769 482
Broadbench Cove . . . . . . .4A 10 SS 214 196
Broadoar Bay . . . . .2E 27 SS 481 468
Broad Sands . . . . .5C 20 SS 468 325
Broomstreet Combe . . . . . .1B 38 SS 815 490
Brownsham . . . . .3D 13 SS 285 259
Brownsham Car Park . . . . .3D 13 SS 284 259
Brownsham Cliff . . . . .2C 12 SS 278 268
. . . . .2E 13 SS 293 263
Brownsham Wood . . . . . . .3E 13 SS 293 259
Brownspear Point . . . . .5D 11 SS 221 235
Bucket Hill . . . . .4B 8 SS 202 086
Buckleigh . . . . .4B 18 SS 432 287
Buck's Cross . . . . .5D 15 SS 348 228
Buck's Down . . . . .4D 15 SS 342 238
Buck's Mills . . . . .4E 15 SS 357 233
Bucks Mills Car Park . . . . .4E 15 SS 357 232
Buck's Wood . . . . .4E 15 SS 355 233
Bude . . . . .6C 8 SS 210 061
Bude, Crescent Car Park . .6B 8 SS 208 061
Bude, Crooklets Car Park
. . . . .5B 8 SS 204 070
Bude Haven . . . . .6B 8 SS 201 065
Bude Lifeboat Station . . . . .6B 8 SS 205 065
Bude, Summerleaze Car Park
. . . . .6B 8 SS 205 065
Bude Tourist Information Centre
. . . . .6B 8 SS 207 061
Bull Point . . . . .2C 26 SS 463 468
Burgundy Chapel . . . . .2C 42 SS 947 481
Burgundy Chapel Combe Car Park
. . . . .3C 42 SS 947 476
Burrow Nose . . . . .1F 29 SS 554 485
The Burton Art Gallery & Museum
. . . . .6D 19 SS 454 269
Butter Hill . . . . .1A 36 SS 748 500

Caffyns Cross . . . . .4B 34 SS 699 474
Caffyns Heanton Down . . . .4A 34 SS 689 471
Capstone Point . . . . .1B 28 SS 519 480
Castle Heritage Centre, Bude
. . . . .6B 8 SS 206 063

Castle Rock . . . . .2C 34 SS 704
Caunter Beach . . . . .4D 9 SS 197
Chambercombe . . . . .2C 28 SS 529
Chambercombe Manor . . . .3D 29 SS 532
Chapel Cross . . . . .6E 41 SS 906
Chapman Rock . . . . .1B 12 SS 262
Cheriton . . . . .5F 35 SS 773
Cherrybridge . . . . .4D 35 SS 713
Cherry Bridge . . . . .4D 35 SS 713
Cherryford Hill . . . . .2E 33 SS 663
Chiselridge Beach . . . . . . .5A 10 SS 211
Chivenor . . . . .3A 22 SS 503
Chivenor Airfield . . . . .3F 21 SS 499
Chivenor Cross . . . . .3A 22 SS 503
Chivenor Ridge . . . . .4A 22 SS 503
Churchtown . . . . .6F 33 SS 679
Clorridge Hill . . . . .3C 30 SS 593
Clovelly . . . . .3A 14 SS 314
Clovelly Bay . . . . .3A 14 SS 320
Clovelly Court Gardens . . . .2A 14 SS 316
Clovelly Cross . . . . .4A 14 SS 318
Clovelly Dykes . . . . .4A 14 SS 311
Clovelly Visitor Centre . . . .3A 14 SS 316
Clovelly Visitor Centre Car Park
. . . . .3A 14 SS 316
Cockington Cliff . . . . .3D 17 SS 403
Coddow Combe . . . . .1B 36 SS 750
Coil Cross . . . . .6D 31 SS 590
Combe Martin . . . . .2B 30 SS 577
Combe Martin Bay . . . . . . .1B 30 SS 576
Combe Martin, Cormelles Car Park
. . . . .3C 30 SS 580
Combe Martin Museum . . .2B 30 SS 577
Combe Martin Tourist Information Centre
. . . . .2B 30 SS 577
Combe Martin Wildlife & Dinosaur Park
. . . . .4D 31 SS 593
Combe Park (Hillsford Bridge) Car Park
. . . . .4F 35 SS 737
Compass Point . . . . .6A 8 SS 199
Coombe . . . . .6E 9 SS 208
Coombe Valley . . . . .6F 9 SS 212
Cornakey Cliff . . . . .1E 9 SS 202
Cornborough Cliff . . . . .1E 17 SS 413
Coscombe . . . . .2F 37 SS 797
Cosgate Hill . . . . .3F 37 SS 797
Cotton Beach . . . . .2D 9 SS 193
Countisbury . . . . .2A 36 SS 747
Countisbury Common . . . . .2C 36 SS 767
Countisbury Cove . . . . .1C 36 SS 747
County Gate . . . . .3F 37 SS 793
County Gate Car Park . . . . .3F 37 SS 793
Cowley Wood Head . . . . . .5C 32 SS 643
Cranford . . . . .6D 15 SS 344
Crawter Hill . . . . .5D 41 SS 899
Crock Point . . . . .2A 34 SS 689
Crooklets Beach . . . . .5B 8 SS 206
Cross . . . . .4E 25 SS 457
Crow Point . . . . .6C 20 SS 465
Croyde . . . . .4D 25 SS 444
Croyde Bay . . . . .4B 24 SS 432
Croyde Beach Car Park . . . .4C 24 SS 435
Croyde Burrows . . . . .4C 24 SS 431
Croyde, Down End Car Park
. . . . .5C 24 SS 441
Croyde, Jones Hill (Village Hall) Car Park
. . . . .4D 25 SS 444
Croyde Sand . . . . .4C 24 SS 431
Culbone . . . . .2E 39 SS 843
Culbone Church . . . . .2E 39 SS 842
Culbone Combe . . . . .2E 39 SS 842
Culbone Hill . . . . .3D 39 SS 836
Culbone Wood . . . . .2C 38 SS 833
Culver Cliff . . . . .3E 43 SS 967
Culver Cliff Sand . . . . .3E 43 SS 967

magehue Rock ... 2C **26** SS 469 468
mehole Point ... 2D **11** SS 222 262
racott ... 6C **10** SS 231 178
an ... 5A **32** SS 629 452
... 4C **34** SS 705 479
an Cross ... 6A **32** SS 625 446
solation Point ... 2E **37** SS 780 499
il's Hole ... 1E **9** SS 204 172
il's Kitchen ... 3B **14** SS 322 245
dywell ... 3D **19** SS 455 298
ston Mill Gardens ... 6E **11** SS 234 227
sworthy Combe ... 2D **37** SS 775 492
erhay Down ... 5C **40** SS 885 452
ery Manor Museum ... 4C **40** SS 888 467
wnland Cross ... 4B **14** SS 327 230
Bridge ... 6B **36** SS 759 454
kpool ... 1A **8** SS 199 114
kpool Car Park ... 6E **9** SS 201 116
Point ... 2B **34** SS 694 496
's Lookout ... 3D **11** SS 224 255

Cleave ... 1C **32** SS 647 492
cott Bridge ... 3A **40** SS 863 471
Down Cross ... 6B **30** SS 570 433
er Close Cross ... 5F **31** SS 615 446
ern Beach ... 2E **35** SS 725 498
ern Brockholes ... 2B **42** SS 930 487
llkerton ... 4D **35** SS 711 470
Lymcove Beach ... 1C **32** SS 645 493
Lyn River ... 4B **36** SS 753 479
the-Water ... 6E **19** SS 463 262
Titchberry Car Park ... 1F **11** SS 244 270
Titchberry Cliff ... 1F **11** SS 246 272
d Beacon ... 6A **8** SS 199 058
n Point ... 1F **11** SS 247 277
Beach ... 2A **8** SS 199 106
mbe ... 6F **43** SS 980 445
cott ... 2C **10** SS 231 215
cott Beach ... 2B **10** SS 220 215
cott Bunkhouse ... 2C **10** SS 231 216
Bay ... 2B **32** SS 632 489
Bay, Glass Box Car Park
... 3A **32** SS 627 479
Bay, Trentishoe Down Car Park
... 3C **32** SS 641 478
Bay, Trentishoe Lane Car Park
... 2B **32** SS 635 480
lle Wood Beach ... 1B **38** SS 811 494
ry Beach ... 4A **10** SS 214 195
ry Beacon ... 4A **10** SS 216 194
ry of River Taw ... 4A **20** SS 439 333
ry of River Torridge ... 4A **20** SS 439 332
nsworthy Car Park ... 2B **12** SS 269 267
nsworthy Cliff ... 1C **12** SS 272 271
or National Park Centre (Lynmouth)
... 2E **35** SS 721 496
or Owl & Hawk Centre
... 3D **41** SS 899 476

Cross ... 5D **17** SS 403 242
Hill ... 6B **36** SS 751 457
tt Cliff ... 1B **12** SS 262 273
tt Cross ... 2B **12** SS 269 262
oint ... 1F **27** SS 494 472
ry ... 5C **8** SS 210 070
orner ... 3F **33** SS 675 475
... 5D **17** SS 408 245
... 4E **25** SS 456 392
reland ... 1B **36** SS 753 508
nd Point ... 1B **36** SS 753 511
gton ... 5B **22** SS 512 323
gton Nature Reserve
... 5B **22** SS 515 327
gton Quay Car Park
... 4B **22** SS 515 332
gton, Tarka Trail Car Park
... 4B **22** SS 517 334
ater Bay ... 1F **27** SS 490 471
ury Brake ... 2B **42** SS 935 483

ry Bower ... 2F **13** SS 304 262
Point ... 3F **15** SS 363 240
n Bridge ... 2A **12** SS 252 266
n Cliff ... 1A **12** SS 252 274
ham ... 4F **25** SS 464 397
ham Car Park ... 4F **25** SS 465 397
Rib ... 2F **37** SS 794 498
wn ... 2E **31** SS 604 479
n Gorge ... 2E **35** SS 722 492
orne Beach ... 1A **38** SS 802 494
orne Pinetum ... 2F **37** SS 793 496
ock ... 1B **36** SS 755 511
Cove ... 2A **30** SS 566 476
re ... 3E **15** SS 350 240
oint ... 2F **39** SS 858 486
ack Hill ... 6E **37** SS 788 457
urland Rocks ... 1E **33** SS 663 495

Great Hangman ... 1E **31** SS 600 480
Greenaleigh Farm ... 3D **43** SS 955 479
Greenaleigh Point ... 2D **43** SS 954 484
Greenaleigh Sand ... 2D **43** SS 951 482
Green Cliff ... 3D **17** SS 405 269
Greencombe Gardens ... 4B **40** SS 877 468
Greenlake Cross ... 6A **12** SS 252 227
Greenway Beach ... 3D **9** SS 196 143
Greenwell Corner ... 3F **33** SS 674 478
Grenville Gate ... 4B **8** SS 209 082
Grunta Beach ... 4B **26** SS 452 448
Grunta Pool ... 4B **26** SS 452 446
Gull Rock ... 1E **9** SS 204 172

Hagginton Hill ... 3F **29** SS 557 469
Hangman Point ... 1C **30** SS 584 482
Hardisworthy Cross ... 3C **10** SS 233 205
Harris Cross ... 6A **14** SS 316 216
Harscott High Cliff ... 5D **9** SS 197 125
Hartland ... 4B **12** SS 260 243
Hartland Abbey & Gardens
... 4F **11** SS 241 249
Hartland Car Park ... 4A **12** SS 259 244
Hartland Cross ... 4B **12** SS 265 242
Hartland Point ... 1D **11** SS 229 277
Hartland Point Car Park ... 1E **11** SS 234 274
Hartland Quay ... 4D **11** SS 222 247
Hartland Quay (Lower) Car Park
... 4D **11** SS 222 247
Hartland Quay Museum ... 4D **11** SS 222 247
Hartland Quay (Upper) Car Park
... 4D **11** SS 225 247
Hawkcombe ... 4C **40** SS 886 461
Hawkcombe Head ... 5E **39** SS 845 457
Hawkcombe Woods National Nature Reserve
... 5A **40** SS 868 456
Hawker's Hut ... 2D **9** SS 198 150
Headon Cross ... 5B **42** SS 935 459
Heale ... 4C **32** SS 645 468
Heale Down ... 4D **33** SS 651 464
Heanton Punchardon ... 2A **22** SS 502 355
Heddon's Mouth ... 1D **33** SS 654 496
Heddon's Mouth Beach ... 1D **33** SS 654 497
Heddon Valley (Hunter's Inn) Car Park
... 2D **33** SS 655 480
Heddon Valley Shop (National Trust)
Information Centre ... 2D **33** SS 655 480
Hele ... 2D **29** SS 534 475
Hele Bay ... 1D **29** SS 538 483
Hele Car Park ... 2D **29** SS 535 477
Hele Corn Mill ... 2D **29** SS 534 474
Henna Cliff ... 2E **9** SS 200 157
Henstridge ... 5C **30** SS 581 448
The Hermitage ... 5A **10** SS 214 182
Higher Clovelly ... 4A **14** SS 311 239
Higher Rowden ... 4C **16** SS 391 250
Higher Sharpnose Point ... 3D **9** SS 194 147
Higher Slade ... 3A **28** SS 506 461
Higher Town ... 4E **43** SS 966 467
Highveer Point ... 1D **33** SS 656 498
Hillsborough Nature Reserve
... 2D **29** SS 531 477
Hillsford Bridge ... 4A **36** SS 740 477
The Hobby ... 3B **14** SS 325 240
The Hobby Drive ... 4C **14** SS 331 235
Holacombe Beach ... 5D **9** SS 197 129
Holdstone Down ... 2F **31** SS 618 479
Holdstone Down Car Park
... 3A **32** SS 623 474
Holdstone Hill ... 2F **31** SS 619 476
Hollerday Hill ... 2D **35** SS 714 497
Hollerday Hill Car Park ... 2C **34** SS 707 497
Hollow Brook ... 1E **33** SS 666 491
Holmer's Combe ... 2C **38** SS 823 485
Hopcott Common ... 6D **43** SS 956 442
Hore Down Gate ... 6D **29** SS 533 439
Horner ... 5D **41** SS 897 454
Horner Car Park ... 5D **41** SS 897 454
Horner Hill ... 6D **41** SS 899 444
Horsey Island ... 4D **21** SS 476 337
Horsey Ridge ... 5D **21** SS 476 329
Hunter's Inn (Heddon Valley) Car Park
... 2D **33** SS 655 480
Huntscott ... 6A **42** SS 924 438
Hurlstone Combe ... 2E **41** SS 901 489
Hurlstone Point ... 1D **41** SS 899 492

Ilfracombe ... 2C **28** SS 521 478
Ilfracombe Aquarium ... 2C **28** SS 524 478
Ilfracombe, Larkstone Car Park
... 2C **28** SS 527 475
Ilfracombe Lifeboat Station
... 2C **28** SS 522 477
Ilfracombe Museum ... 2B **28** SS 517 478
Ilfracombe Tourist Information Centre
... 2B **28** SS 518 477
Ilfracombe Tunnels Beaches
... 2B **28** SS 515 477

Inkerman Bridge ... 2F **33** SS 677 486
Instow ... 2F **19** SS 472 304
Instow Barton Marsh ... 6D **21** SS 476 319
Instow, Sandhills Car Park
... 1F **19** SS 474 311
Instow Sands ... 1E **19** SS 469 310
Instow Signal Box ... 2F **19** SS 473 301
Iron Letters Cross ... 5D **29** SS 537 443
Isley Marsh Nature Reserve
... 5E **21** SS 489 328

James's Cross ... 2F **9** SS 215 151

Keivill's Wood ... 4E **15** SS 350 236
Kennerland Cross ... 6B **14** SS 327 217
Kentisbury ... 6F **31** SS 622 438
Kenwith Valley Nature Reserve
... 5C **18** SS 446 272
Kernstone Cross ... 5E **11** SS 236 233
Killington Cross ... 5F **33** SS 672 456
Killington Lane Station, Lynton &
Barnstaple Railway ... 5F **33** SS 670 458
King's Cross ... 5C **10** SS 238 183
King William's Bridge ... 6E **9** SS 208 116
Kipling Tors ... 4A **18** SS 422 288
Kipscombe Combe ... 1B **36** SS 759 502
Kipscombe Cross ... 2C **36** SS 761 491
Kipscombe Hill ... 2C **36** SS 764 493
Kitstone Hill ... 3E **29** SS 543 462
Knap Down ... 2D **31** SS 592 470
Knap Head ... 5A **10** SS 210 187
Knotty Corner ... 4E **17** SS 411 251
Knowle Top ... 6F **41** SS 913 444
Knowlwater Bridge ... 1C **22** SS 520 361

Lake ... 6F **23** SS 554 316
Leat Meadow ... 6B **22** SS 511 319
Lee ... 2E **27** SS 484 463
Lee Bay ... 2D **27** SS 479 469
... 2B **34** SS 691 494
Lee Bay (Lynton) Car Park
... 2B **34** SS 695 491
Lee Cross ... 4E **27** SS 488 441
Leeford ... 3D **37** SS 770 481
Lee Hills ... 3F **29** SS 551 466
Lester Cliff ... 2B **30** SS 579 475
Lester Point ... 2B **30** SS 575 476
Ley Hill ... 5C **40** SS 889 451
Lighthouse Cross ... 4E **13** SS 291 243
Lincombe ... 3F **27** SS 498 459
Lithytree Stile ... 5F **11** SS 247 232
Litter Mouth ... 1E **9** SS 207 169
Little Black Hill ... 6E **37** SS 782 457
Littleham Cross ... 6F **17** SS 430 239
Little Hangman ... 1C **30** SS 585 480
Long Bridge ... 5F **23** SS 557 329
Lower Bight of Fernham ... 3C **14** SS 333 240
Lower Sharpnose Point ... 5D **9** SS 195 126
Lower Slade ... 4B **28** SS 512 459
Luccombe ... 6F **41** SS 911 446
Luccombe Mill Bridge ... 6F **41** SS 916 442
Lucky Hole ... 2D **9** SS 196 151
Lyn & Exmoor Museum ... 2E **35** SS 720 493
Lyn Bridge ... 3D **35** SS 719 485
Lynbridge ... 3D **35** SS 718 487
Lynch Bridge ... 3E **41** SS 900 476
Lyn Cross ... 4E **35** SS 728 479
Lyn Down ... 4E **35** SS 724 470
Lyn Model Railway ... 2E **35** SS 723 493
Lyn Mouth ... 1E **35** SS 722 500
Lynmouth ... 2E **35** SS 724 493
Lynmouth Bay ... 2F **35** SS 732 499
Lynton ... 2D **35** SS 718 494
Lynton & Barnstaple Railway
Killington Lane Station ... 5F **33** SS 670 458
Woody Bay Station ... 5A **34** SS 682 464
Lynton & Lynmouth Cliff Railway
... 2E **35** SS 720 496
Lynton Cross ... 6D **29** SS 538 437
Lynton Tourist Information Centre
... 2D **35** SS 718 495

Maer ... 5B **8** SS 207 079
Maer Cliff ... 4B **8** SS 201 080
Maer Down ... 5B **8** SS 202 076
Maer Lake Nature Reserve
... 5B **8** SS 207 075
Malmsmead ... 4F **37** SS 791 477
Malmsmead Hill ... 5E **37** SS 786 464
Malmsmead, Lorna Doone Road Car Park
... 4F **37** SS 791 477
Mannacott Lane Head ... 3E **33** SS 665 479
Mansley Cliff ... 2B **10** SS 224 217
Marsland Beach ... 1E **9** SS 207 172
Marsland Cliff ... 1E **9** SS 208 171
Marsland Mouth ... 6A **10** SS 211 174

Marsland Valley Nature Reserve
.............6B **10** SS 225 172
Martinhoe ....2E **33** SS 667 486
Martinhoe Common ....3F **33** SS 677 475
Martinhoe Cross ....5A **34** SS 684 463
Mattocks Down ....6E **31** SS 602 436
Mead ....6B **10** SS 221 177
Menachurch Point ......4B **8** SS 200 088
Mermaid's Pool ....1E **17** SS 417 289
Middleborough Hill ....4C **24** SS 431 399
Middlecombe Cross .....5D **43** SS 951 457
Milford ....6E **11** SS 232 226
Milford Cross ....1C **10** SS 232 220
Milky Way Adventure Park
.............5B **14** SS 326 228
Mill Hill ....5C **38** SS 827 452
Minehead ....4F **43** SS 973 463
Minehead Bluff ....1F **41** SS 914 493
Minehead Lifeboat Station
.............3F **43** SS 970 471
Minehead, Moor Wood Car Park
.............3D **43** SS 954 474
Minehead, North Hill Car Park
.............3C **42** SS 942 473
Minehead, Quay West Car Park
.............3E **43** SS 969 471
Minehead, Reservoir Car Park
.............4D **43** SS 958 469
Minehead Station ......4F **43** SS 974 463
Minehead Tourist Information Centre
.............4F **43** SS 973 463
Minehead Youth Hostel .6F **43** SS 972 442
Minniemoor Cross ......6D **33** SS 658 446
Moreton Park ....6B **18** SS 433 261
Morte Bay ....5A **26** SS 441 430
Mortehoe ....3B **26** SS 457 451
Mortehoe Car Park .....3B **26** SS 458 451
Mortehoe Museum ....3B **26** SS 457 452
Morte Point ....3A **26** SS 440 455
Morte Stone ....3A **26** SS 438 456
Morwenstow ....2E **9** SS 205 152
Morwenstow Church Car Park
.............2E **9** SS 206 152
Mouth Mill ....2E **13** SS 298 265
Mouthmill Beach ....2E **13** SS 295 265
Muddlebridge ....5C **22** SS 524 325
Mullacott Camping Barn .4B **28** SS 513 452
Mullacott Cross ....5B **28** SS 511 444
Museum of Barnstaple & North Devon
.............5F **23** SS 558 329

Nabor Point ....3A **10** SS 214 202
Napps Cliff ....3D **25** SS 442 406
Natcott ....5C **12** SS 279 237
Netherton Cross ....2C **30** SS 588 470
New Bridge ....4D **41** SS 899 466
Newquay Ridge ....3E **19** SS 467 298
Newthorne Beach ....4A **10** SS 213 192
Newton Cross ....5F **11** SS 245 236
Northam ....3C **18** SS 449 291
Northam Burrows (Beach) Car Park
.............3B **18** SS 434 297
Northam Burrows Country Park
.............2C **18** SS 445 308
Northam Burrows (Country Park) Car Park
.............1C **18** SS 448 310
Northam Burrows (Golf Club) Car Park
.............2B **18** SS 438 305
North Bridge ....2D **41** SS 898 480
North Cleave ....2B **32** SS 636 484
North Cliff ....1E **11** SS 236 275
North Common ....3B **38** SS 815 470
Northcott Mouth ....4B **8** SS 202 084
Northcott Mouth Car Park
.............4B **8** SS 203 084
North Devon Maritime Museum
.............2E **19** SS 463 304
North Hill ....2C **42** SS 940 480

Oare ....3A **38** SS 801 473
Oare Common ....6F **37** SS 798 459
Oareford ....4B **38** SS 813 463
Old Burrow Hill ....2E **37** SS 785 493
Old Mill Leat ....6A **10** SS 216 174
Ora Hill ....4D **25** SS 446 395
Oreweed Cove ....3B **26** SS 454 458
Ossaborough ....5E **27** SS 481 434
Outer Appledore Rocks .2D **27** SS 478 468
Oxford Cross ....3F **25** SS 469 407

Parracombe ....6E **33** SS 668 448
Parracombe Lane Head ..5F **33** SS 672 453
Pattard Bridge ....4B **12** SS 261 249
Pattard Cross ....3A **12** SS 257 256
Pebble Ridge Adventure Golf & Go Karts
.............3B **18** SS 433 294
Penhill Point ....3B **22** SS 517 343

Peppercombe ....6B **16** SS 383 238
Peppercombe Castle ....5B **16** SS 381 241
Periton ....5D **43** SS 958 458
Periton Cross ....5D **43** SS 955 456
Periton Hill ....6D **43** SS 950 447
Peter Rock ....1D **33** SS 651 493
Philham ....6A **12** SS 257 224
Philham Cross ....6A **12** SS 257 227
Pickwell ....3E **25** SS 456 409
Pickwell Down ....2F **25** SS 461 412
Pillhead Bridge ....5F **19** SS 476 272
Pilton ....3F **23** SS 555 341
Pimpley Bridge ....3C **18** SS 443 299
Pippacott ....1C **22** SS 528 371
Pittcombe Head ....4E **39** SS 841 462
Pitt Cross ....3A **12** SS 250 258
Pool Bridge ....6B **40** SS 875 447
Pool Cross ....6B **40** SS 871 442
Porlock ....4C **40** SS 886 467
Porlock Bay ....2B **40** SS 873 488
Porlock Beach ....3A **40** SS 869 476
Porlock, Central Car Park ...4C **40** SS 885 468
Porlock Common ....5E **39** SS 848 459
Porlock Common Car Park
.............4E **39** SS 845 461
Porlockford Bridge ....3A **40** SS 867 473
Porlock Hill ....4B **40** SS 875 462
Porlock Visitor Centre ..4C **40** SS 884 467
Porlock Weir ....3A **40** SS 864 478
Porlock Weir Car Park ..3A **40** SS 864 478
Potter's Hill ....6B **26** SS 458 429
Pottington ....4F **23** SS 550 335
Prixford ....1E **23** SS 548 367
Pully Ridge ....5A **20** SS 448 323
Putsborough ....3D **25** SS 448 402
Putsborough Sand ......2D **25** SS 446 410
Putsborough Sands Car Park
.............3D **25** SS 447 407

Ramsey Beach ....1C **32** SS 646 493
Rane Beach ....4D **9** SS 197 131
Rane Head ....4D **9** SS 198 132
The Rawn's ....1D **31** SS 593 482
Rawn's Rocks ....1D **31** SS 594 485
Rectory Close Cross ...2F **21** SS 495 354
Red Cleave ....1F **31** SS 617 483
Red Post ....4D **41** SS 896 465
Rhydda Bank Cross .....3C **32** SS 642 479
Rickard's Down ....5A **18** SS 423 272
Rillage Point ....1E **29** SS 541 486
River Caen ....3E **21** SS 481 341
River Taw ....4D **23** SS 533 339
River Torridge ....4D **19** SS 459 286
Roadway Corner ....1F **25** SS 466 423
Robber's Bridge ....4B **38** SS 819 464
Robber's Bridge Car Park ..4C **38** SS 821 464
Rockford ....4B **36** SS 756 477
Rockham Bay ....2B **26** SS 451 460
Rockham Beach ....2B **26** SS 456 461
Roundswell ....6E **23** SS 544 316
Round Tree Corner .....4F **11** SS 246 240
Rugged Jack ....2C **34** SS 705 497

St Catherine's Tor ....4D **11** SS 224 241
St Morwenna's Well ....2D **9** SS 197 154
Saltpill Duck Pond ....4A **22** SS 504 330
Samson's Bay ....1E **29** SS 545 485
Sandhole Cliff ....3B **10** SS 221 209
Sandhole Cross ....2B **10** SS 224 210
Sandy Bay ....2A **30** SS 568 474
Sandymere ....2B **18** SS 438 307
Sandy Mouth ....2B **8** SS 201 100
Sandy Mouth Beach .....2B **8** SS 200 101
Sandy Mouth Car Park ..2B **8** SS 203 100
Saunton ....6E **25** SS 456 376
Saunton Beach Car Park .6D **25** SS 447 376
Saunton Down ....5C **24** SS 438 382
Saunton Down Car Park ..5D **25** SS 440 380
Saunton Sands ....2A **20** SS 441 355
Scob Hill ....5B **36** SS 752 466
Scobhill Road Car Park .5A **36** SS 745 468
Screda Cove ....4D **11** SS 222 244
Screda Point ....4D **11** SS 220 242
Selworthy ....4F **41** SS 919 468
Selworthy Beacon ......3F **41** SS 918 479
Selworthy Beacon Car Park
.............3B **42** SS 930 476
Selworthy Church Car Park
.............4F **41** SS 919 467
Selworthy Sand ....1E **41** SS 908 492
Seven Ash Cross ....5E **31** SS 609 446
Seven Hills ....2A **28** SS 509 474
Shag Point ....1E **27** SS 486 471
Shamley Bridge ....2F **11** SS 246 267
Shamley Bridge Cross ..2F **11** SS 246 268
Sherrycombe ....2E **31** SS 608 476
Shillett Wood Car Park .4A **40** SS 861 460
Shilstone Hill ....6B **36** SS 759 459

Shilstone Hill (1) Car Park
.............5B **36** SS 753 4
Shilstone Hill (2) Car Park
.............5B **36** SS 753 4
Shilstone Hill (3) Car Park
.............6B **36** SS 753 4
Shilstone Hill (4) Car Park
.............6B **36** SS 755
Shilstone Hill (5) Car Park
.............6B **36** SS 758
Shipload Bay ....1F **11** SS 244
Silcombe Combe ....3D **39** SS 832
Silford Cross ....4B **18** SS 435
Sillery Sands ....2F **35** SS 738
Sir Robert's Chair ....1E **37** SS 780
Sister's Fountain .....2F **37** SS 792
Skern ....2D **19** SS 453
Slade Lane Cross ......6A **32** SS 620
Sloo Wood ....6A **16** SS 373
Smallcombe Bridge .....4F **35** SS 732
Smythen Cross ....6A **30** SS 562
South Common ....6A **38** SS 805
South Dean Corner .....2C **32** SS 641
Southern Ball ....4E **37** SS 784
South Hole ....3B **10** SS 220
South West Coast Path
Bude ....6B **8** SS 205
Minehead ....4F **43** SS 971
South West Coast Path Monument
.............4F **43** SS 971
Sparhanger Cross ......5D **35** SS 719
Speke's Mill Mouth ....5D **11** SS 222
Springfield Cross .....2E **23** SS 542
Spur Cross ....5B **12** SS 265
Stanbury Beach ....4D **9** SS 197
Stanbury Cross ....3F **9** SS 212
Stanbury Mouth ....4D **9** SS 199
Steeple Point ....6D **9** SS 198
Sterridge Valley ......4F **29** SS 554
Sticklepath ....5E **23** SS 544
Stock Common ....6E **35** SS 725
Stoke ....4E **11** SS 236
Stonecombe ....6E **31** SS 600
Stoneditch Hill ....4C **30** SS 585
Stony Corner ....3F **31** SS 613
Stowe Cliffs ....2B **8** SS 202
Straypark Corner ......4A **36** SS 743
Submarine Forest ......3A **40** SS 867
Sugarloaf Hill ....1A **38** SS 800
Summer House Hill .....3E **35** SS 722
Swanpool Marsh Nature Reserve
.............1D **21** SS 47
Swansford Hill ....5D **11** SS 22
Syncock's Cross ....5F **19** SS 47

Tapeley Park & Gardens ...3F **19** SS 47
Taw Bridge ....4F **23** SS 55
Tense Rocks ....1D **11** SS 22
Tidna Shute ....3D **9** SS 19
Tippacott ....4C **36** SS 76
Tippacott Ridge ....5D **37** SS 77
Titchberry ....1F **11** SS 24
Tivington ....5B **42** SS 93
Tivington Cross ....5B **42** SS 93
Torridge Bridge ....5D **19** SS 45
Torrs Park ....2A **28** SS 50
Torrs Point ....2A **28** SS 50
Tourist Information Centre
Barnstaple ....5F **23** SS 55
Bideford ....6D **19** SS 45
Braunton ....1E **21** SS 48
Bude ....6B **8** SS 20
Combe Martin ....2B **30** SS 5
Ilfracombe ....2B **28** SS 5
Lynton ....2D **35** SS 7
Minehead ....4F **43** SS 97
Woolacombe ....5B **26** SS 4
Trayne Hills ....3D **29** SS 5
Trentishoe ....2C **32** SS 6
Trentishoe Down ....3A **32** SS 6
Trimstone ....5F **27** SS 4
Turnpike Cross ....5E **27** SS 4
Twitchen Cross ....6A **28** SS 5
Twitchin Combe ....2B **38** SS 8
Two Pots ....5D **29** SS 5

Ulfred Point ....2E **27** SS 4
Ultimate Adventure Centre
.............6B **18** SS 4
Upright Cliff ....2D **11** SS 2

The Valley of Rocks ...2C **34** SS 7
The Valley of Rocks Car Park
.............2D **35** SS 7
Velator ....2E **21** SS 4
Velator Bridge ....2E **21** SS 4
Velator Quay ....2E **21** SS 4

...............4E **13** SS 293 242
ford Cross ....5B **42** SS 931 458
age Cliff ....2D **9** SS 199 151
r Centre, Clovelly ....3A **14** SS 315 249
r Centre, Porlock .....4C **40** SS 884 467

en Cliff ....3D **11** SS 225 252
en Gutter ....1B **8** SS 201 110
en Little Beach ....2A **8** SS 199 108
en Long Beach ....2A **8** SS 199 104
en Point ....1B **8** SS 201 113
or's Bridge ....6E **11** SS 238 225
Mouth ....1F **29** SS 553 482
mouth Castle ....1F **29** SS 555 480
smeet ....3A **36** SS 743 486
smeet Car Park .....3A **36** SS 743 487
mbe ....5B **10** SS 228 183
mbe Mouth ....5A **10** SS 211 180

........6A **10** SS 213 179
cott Cliff ....4C **16** SS 396 257
Appledore ....2E **19** SS 463 309
ott Brake Car Park ..4F **39** SS 853 463
rn Beach ....2E **35** SS 721 499
rn Brockholes ....2F **41** SS 917 489
lkerton Common ...5B **34** SS 695 465
eigh ....4F **19** SS 471 286
Luccombe ....4D **41** SS 899 462
Lymcove Beach ...1C **32** SS 644 491
Lyn ....3E **35** SS 724 482
Lynch ....3E **41** SS 901 476
Lyn River ....6D **35** SS 717 458
Porlock ....3B **40** SS 870 470
Somerset Railway ....4F **43** SS 974 463
Titchberry Cliff .....1F **11** SS 240 274
vard Ho! ....3A **18** SS 429 291
vard Ho!, Main Car Park
..................3B **18** SS 432 292

Westward Ho!, Seafield (Kipling Tors) Car Park
..................3A **18** SS 423 290
Westward Ho!, Slipway Car Park
..................3B **18** SS 433 294
Wheatham Combe ....1A **38** SS 809 491
Wheel Cross ....5B **30** SS 578 446
Wheeler's Stone ....2B **24** SS 429 412
White Cross ....4D **43** SS 959 464
Whiting Cove ....3B **26** SS 450 458
Whiting Hole ....2B **24** SS 422 410
Whitstone Post ....4F **39** SS 856 462
Whitstone Post Car Park
..................4F **39** SS 855 462
Whit Stones ....4F **39** SS 853 462
Widmouth Head ....1E **29** SS 548 486
Widmouth Hill ....2E **29** SS 545 475
Wild Pear Beach ....2C **30** SS 580 477
Willingcott Cross ....5E **27** SS 485 431
Willingcott Cross Car Park
..................5E **27** SS 485 431
Wilsham ....3B **36** SS 756 484
Windbury Head ....2D **13** SS 286 266
Windbury Point ....2D **13** SS 286 267
Windcutter Hill ....3E **27** SS 486 456
Wind Hill ....2F **35** SS 739 492
Windy Cross ....2C **22** SS 523 355
Windypost Cross ....4E **35** SS 722 478
Wingate Combe ....2D **37** SS 779 495
Withy Combe ....2D **39** SS 837 480
Woodcombe ....4D **43** SS 954 464
Woodford ....4F **9** SS 219 134
Woodford Cross ....3F **9** SS 219 142
Woodtown ....6E **17** SS 413 235
Woody Bay ....1F **33** SS 678 493
..................2F **33** SS 672 487
Woody Bay, Cherryford Hill Car Park
..................2F **33** SS 674 484
Woody Bay, Inkerman Bridge Car Park
..................2F **33** SS 676 486

Woody Bay Station Car Park
..................5A **34** SS 683 463
Woody Bay Station, Lynton &
Barnstaple Railway .....5A **34** SS 682 464
Woolacombe ....5B **26** SS 458 437
Woolacombe Down ......1F **25** SS 460 423
Woolacombe, Esplanade Car Park
..................5B **26** SS 457 437
Woolacombe Sand ....6B **26** SS 452 425
Woolacombe, Sandy Burrows Car Park
..................5B **26** SS 458 434
Woolacombe Tourist Information Centre
..................5B **26** SS 457 438
Woolacombe Warren ...1E **25** SS 454 421
Woolhanger Common
..................5B **34** SS 690 460
Wootton Common ....6C **42** SS 946 440
Worlington Cross ....2F **19** SS 480 305
Worthy ....2F **39** SS 858 481
Worthy Combe ....3F **39** SS 855 478
Worthygate Wood ....4F **15** SS 363 237
Worthy Wood ....3F **39** SS 858 478
Wrafton ....2F **21** SS 491 355
Wrangle Point ....5A **8** SS 199 072
..................5B **8** SS 201 072
Wren Beach ....5D **9** SS 198 121
Wringcliff Bay ....2C **34** SS 701 498

Yapham Cross ....3D **13** SS 283 250
Yearnor Mill Bridge ....3F **39** SS 851 472
Yearnor Wood ....2F **39** SS 853 481
Yelland ....5F **21** SS 493 321
Yenworthy Combe ......1A **38** SS 802 492
Yenworthy Common .....2A **38** SS 806 480
Yeol Mouth ....1E **9** SS 202 163
Yeolmouth Cliff ....1E **9** SS 203 161
Yeo Vale Bridge ....6F **17** SS 421 234
Youltree Cross ....3B **12** SS 262 257

South West Coast Path - Route Planner

Bude to Minehead

Key: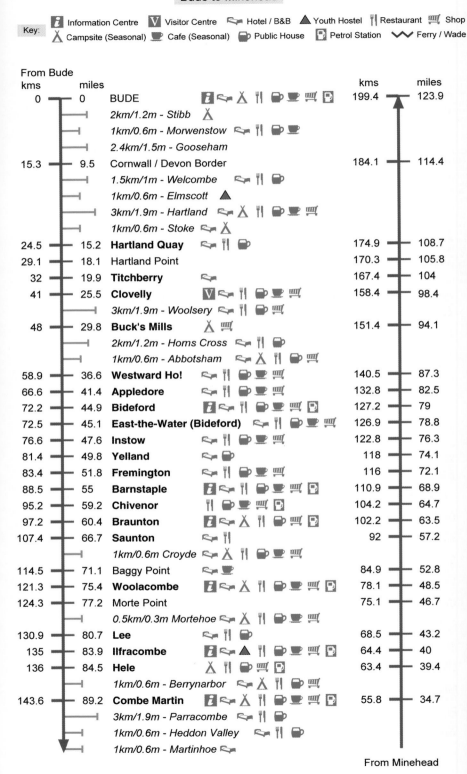

| | Information Centre | | Visitor Centre | Hotel / B&B | Youth Hostel | Restaurant | Shop |
| Campsite (Seasonal) | Cafe (Seasonal) | Public House | Petrol Station | Ferry / Wade |

From Bude

kms	miles			kms	miles
0	0	**BUDE**		199.4	123.9
		2km/1.2m - Stibb			
		1km/0.6m - Morwenstow			
		2.4km/1.5m - Gooseham			
15.3	9.5	Cornwall / Devon Border		184.1	114.4
		1.5km/1m - Welcombe			
		1km/0.6m - Elmscott			
		3km/1.9m - Hartland			
		1km/0.6m - Stoke			
24.5	15.2	**Hartland Quay**		174.9	108.7
29.1	18.1	Hartland Point		170.3	105.8
32	19.9	**Titchberry**		167.4	104
41	25.5	**Clovelly**		158.4	98.4
		3km/1.9m - Woolsery			
48	29.8	**Buck's Mills**		151.4	94.1
		2km/1.2m - Horns Cross			
		1km/0.6m - Abbotsham			
58.9	36.6	**Westward Ho!**		140.5	87.3
66.6	41.4	**Appledore**		132.8	82.5
72.2	44.9	**Bideford**		127.2	79
72.5	45.1	**East-the-Water (Bideford)**		126.9	78.8
76.6	47.6	**Instow**		122.8	76.3
81.4	49.8	**Yelland**		118	74.1
83.4	51.8	**Fremington**		116	72.1
88.5	55	**Barnstaple**		110.9	68.9
95.2	59.2	**Chivenor**		104.2	64.7
97.2	60.4	**Braunton**		102.2	63.5
107.4	66.7	**Saunton**		92	57.2
		1km/0.6m Croyde			
114.5	71.1	**Baggy Point**		84.9	52.8
121.3	75.4	**Woolacombe**		78.1	48.5
124.3	77.2	Morte Point		75.1	46.7
		0.5km/0.3m Mortehoe			
130.9	80.7	**Lee**		68.5	43.2
135	83.9	**Ilfracombe**		64.4	40
136	84.5	**Hele**		63.4	39.4
		1km/0.6m - Berrynarbor			
143.6	89.2	**Combe Martin**		55.8	34.7
		3km/1.9m - Parracombe			
		1km/0.6m - Heddon Valley			
		1km/0.6m - Martinhoe			

From Minehead

From Bude				From Minehead
kms	miles		kms	miles
		1km/0.6m - Martinhoe 🛏		
159.5	99.1	**Woody Bay**	39.9	24.8
165	102.5	**Lynton**	34.4	21.4
165.7	103	**Lynmouth**	33.7	20.9
168	104.4	**Countisbury**	31.4	19.5
182.3	113.3	**Culbone**	17.1	10.6
185.1	115	**Porlock Weir**	14.3	8.9
		1km/0.6m -Porlock		
		1.5km/0.9m -Allerford		
189.7	117.9	**Bossington**	9.7	6
199.4	123.9	MINEHEAD	0	0

- Most campsites and caravan sites are seasonal and may not be open in the winter, check before going.
- Some caravan sites are for Caravan Club members only, check before going.
- Some cafes and beach shops are only open in summer.

Ferry Information

Ferry	From	To	Reference	Frequency
Torridge Estuary	**Appledore** 〰 **Instow**		2E **19** (SS 468 303)	

Operator: Instow to Appledore Ferry, Tel: 07757 620999
www.appledoreinstowferry.com/
Early April - Late October, 2 hours either side of high tide.
Alternatives - official path via Bideford Long Bridge
- A386 (9km / 5.5miles)

Tourist Information Centres

Name	Address	Telephone
Barnstaple	Museum of Barnstaple, The Square. EX32 8LN	01271 375000
Bideford	Burton Art Gallery, Kingsley Road, Bideford. EX39 2QQ	01237 477676
Braunton	Caen Street, Braunton. EX33 1AA	01271 816688
Bude	The Crescent, Bude. EX23 8LE	01288 354240
Clovelly	Clovelly, Near Bideford. EX39 5TA	01237 431781
Combe Martin	Cross Street, Combe Martin. EX34 0DH	01271 889031
Ilfracombe	Landmark Thtre, The Seafront, Ilfracombe. EX34 9BZ	01271 863001
Lynton	Lynton Town Hall, Lee Road, Lynton. EX35 6BT	01598 752225
Minehead	The Avenue, Minehead. TA24 5AP	01643 702624
Porlock	West End, Porlock. TA24 8QD	01643 863150
Woolacombe	The Esplanade, Woolacombe. EX34 7DL	01271 870553

Safety & Security when walking

General

- Make sure you are wearing appropriate clothing and footwear, with suitable extra clothing in case the weather changes, or if you get delayed or misjudge how long it will take you to complete the walk.
- Be careful, if you are inexperienced, not to undertake a walk that is too ambitious.
- Take plenty to eat and drink, there are not always opportunities to buy extra provisions.
- Be sure someone knows where you are going and when to expect you back. Let them know when you have returned as well.
- Although taking a mobile phone is a good idea, in some remote areas there may not be a signal and therefore should not be relied upon.
- When walking on roads follow the advice in the Highway Code.
- Always use a pavement and safe crossing points whenever possible.
- Where there is no pavement it is better to walk on the right hand side of the road, facing oncoming traffic.
- Only cross railway lines at designated places and never walk along railway lines.
- Good navigational skills and a compass are essential.
- Always take warm and waterproof clothing; conditions at coastal locations can always change quickly, even in summer.
- Walking boots should always be worn.
- Gloves and headgear are advisable too in cold weather.
- Other essentials to take are; a waterproof backpack, "high energy" foods, a whistle, a torch (with spare batteries and bulb), a watch, a first aid kit, water purification tablets and a survival bag.
- Ready made first aid kits are available with all necessary items included.
- High factor sunscreen should be used in sunny weather, the sun can be particularly strong and can be hidden by sea breezes. Sunglasses are advisable too.
- Informal paths leading to beaches can be dangerous and are best avoided.
- When crossing a beach, make sure you know the tide times to avoid being cut off.
- Some cliffs overhang or are unstable and these are not always obvious.
- On the coast, mist, fog and high winds are more likely and can be hazardous.

The international distress signal is six blasts of a whistle repeated at one minute intervals (the reply is three) or six flashes of light at one minute intervals (again the reply is three). In an emergency dial 999 or 112.

The Countryside Code

- Be safe - plan ahead and follow any signs.
  Even when going out locally, it's best to get the latest information about where and when you can go; for example, your rights to go onto some areas of open land may be restricted while work is carried out, for safety reasons or during breeding seasons. Follow advice and local signs, and be prepared for the unexpected.
- Leave gates and property as you find them.
  Please respect the working life of the countryside, as our actions can affect people's livelihoods, our heritage, and the safety and welfare of animals and ourselves.
- Protect plants and animals, and take your litter home.
  We have a responsibility to protect our countryside now and for future generations, so make sure you don't harm animals, birds, plants, or trees. Fires can be as devastating to wildlife and habitats as they are to people and property.
- Keep dogs under close control.
  The countryside is a great place to exercise dogs, but it's every owner's duty to make sure their dog is not a danger or nuisance to farm animals, wildlife or other people.
- Consider other people.
  Showing consideration and respect for other people makes the countryside a pleasant environment for everyone - at home, at work and at leisure.

Useful Information

 Tide Times

Information on Tide Times
www.tidetimes.org.uk
includes sunrise and sunset times

Weather

Met Office
www.metoffice.gov.uk

 Countryside Access

For more information visit
www.naturalengland.org.uk

OS Map Reading

OS Map reading made easy
PDF download

 OS National Grid

OS Using the National Grid
PDF download

Danger Areas

Public access to military areas
www.gov.uk/guidance/public-access-to-military-areas

 Traveline South West

SW Public Transport Information
www.travelinesw.com
Getting from A to B by public transport

UKcampsite

Comprehensive campsite directory
for campers and caravanners
www.ukcampsite.co.uk